B
CLI (dupli) 15⁰⁰
Cwiklik, Robt.
AUTHOR
Bill Clinton
TITLE

B
CLI Cwiklik, Robt.
C
Bill Clinton

Our 42nd President

BILL CLINTON

by Robert Cwiklik

The Millbrook Press
Brookfield, Connecticut
A Gateway Biography

Cover photograph courtesy of AP/Wide World
Background cover photograph courtesy of Reuters/Bettmann
Photographs courtesy of Reuters/Bettmann: pp. 4, 38 (top),
41, 42; Gamma Liaison: pp. 7 (both), 10 (bottom), 18, 31
(Cynthia Johnson), 38 (bottom, Brad Markel); Sygma: pp. 10
(top), 15, 24; UPI/Bettmann: pp. 21, 28, 35 (both);
AP/Wide World: p. 45

Map courtesy of Blackbirch Graphics

Library of Congress Cataloging-in-Publication Data
Cwiklik, Robert.
Bill Clinton : our 42nd president / Robert Cwiklik.
p. cm. — (A Gateway biography)
Includes bibliographical references and index.
Summary: A brief biography of the forty-second president of the
United States, highlighting his political life and his successful
1992 campaign against President Bush.
ISBN 1-56294-387-1 (lib. bdg.)
1. Clinton, Bill, 1946-   —Juvenile literature. 2. Presidents—
United States—Biography—Juvenile literature. 3. Presidents—
United States—Election—1992—Juvenile literature. [1. Clinton,
Bill, 1946-   . 2. Presidents.] I. Title. II. Series
E886.C86 1993
973.929′092—dc20   [B]   92-43159   CIP   AC

Published by The Millbrook Press
2 Old New Milford Road
Brookfield, Connecticut 06804

Bill Clinton

Bill Clinton, the Democrats' nominee for president, prepares to give his acceptance speech at their convention in New York City.

On *Thursday, July 16, 1992,* Bill Clinton, governor of Arkansas, walked onto the stage at Madison Square Garden in New York City. The arena was packed with thousands of people for the national convention of the Democratic Party. All eyes were on Clinton as he stepped up to accept the nomination of his party for the presidency of the United States.

The nation was also watching. Millions would see Clinton's speech on television. In November he would run against President George Bush to see which man voters would elect as their president for the next four years.

Clinton, a handsome forty-five-year-old, was much younger than the president, although his bushy brown hair had gone mostly gray. In his speech, he asked Americans to choose a "new generation" of leaders. He promised to fight for the "forgotten" people, those "who do the work, pay the taxes, raise the kids and play by the rules."

Voters seemed to like Clinton's call to the "forgotten middle class." After the convention, he surged ahead of Bush in the polls. But there were still months to go before the election, and Americans did not often vote out sitting presidents. Clinton braced for the fight of his life.

Bill Clinton's father, William Jefferson Blythe III, a car salesman, and his mother, Virginia Cassidy, a nurse, were married in 1941 in Shreveport, Louisiana. Blythe was in the service during World War II. When he came home, the best job he could find was selling heavy equipment in far-off Chicago. Virginia stayed behind, and when she found she was pregnant moved in with her parents in the small town of Hope, Arkansas. Blythe made the long drive there to see his family whenever he could. But one tragic night, his car crashed into a ditch and he was killed. Three months later, on August 19, 1946, Virginia gave birth to a son. She named him William Jefferson Blythe IV, after the father he would never meet.

Virginia needed training for a better-paying job, so she would be able to support herself and her baby. She left little "Billy" with her parents while she studied in New Orleans to become a nurse-

Bill at eighteen months, and . . .

. . . as a four-year-old Arkansas cowboy.

anesthetist. Bill's grandparents owned a grocery store in a poor section of Hope. They were not well educated, but they saw the value of learning and discipline. They taught Bill to count and to read. When he was in first grade, he was already reading the newspaper.

In 1950, Virginia married Roger Clinton, a car salesman. When Bill was seven, the family moved to Hot Springs, Arkansas. The boy was known as Bill Clinton by classmates, although he did not legally change his name until he was a teenager. He was an excellent student, always eager to learn. Sometimes teachers found him too eager. He once got a D in conduct because, his teacher said, he always knew the answers in class and did not give others a chance to speak.

But while Bill's future as a student was bright, there were dark days at home. Roger Clinton drank heavily and had a hot temper. When he was drunk he sometimes hit his wife and the child they had together, Roger, Jr., born when Bill was ten. During one tantrum, he fired a gun in the house. One day, when Bill was fourteen years old, his patience ran out. Roger senior was drunk and bullying Virginia and Roger, Jr. Bill stepped into his path. "You'll never hit either of them again," he said sternly. "If you want them, you'll have to go through me." Roger Clinton's violence against his family stopped.

The adults around Bill noticed early on that he was a natural leader among his classmates. He was elected president of his junior class in high school. At seventeen, he attended Boys State, a camp where students learned about politics. Bill was elected a delegate to Boys Nation, a gathering of teenagers from around the country in Washington, D.C. The group visited the White House, where Bill shook hands with his hero, President John F. Kennedy. That handshake changed Bill Clinton's life. He had been trying to decide on a career. After meeting Kennedy, he knew, as his mother put it, that "politics was the answer for him."

Music was also a big part of Bill's life. He played the saxophone and helped form a three-piece jazz band called Three Blind Mice. He was also a leader in the high school band. But he still found time to

Bill met his hero, President John F. Kennedy, on a trip to the White House with the Boys Nation youth group.

A triumphant-looking Bill on his high school graduation day.

excel in his studies. He became a National Merit Scholarship semifinalist and graduated fourth in his class of 323. Carolyn Staley, a friend from high school, said that in everything Bill did, "he had to be the best."

Bill was offered a scholarship to study music in college. Instead, he went to Georgetown University, in Washington, D.C., to study international affairs. There he buckled down to prepare for a life in politics.

At Georgetown, Bill Clinton met students and teachers "from all over the country and all over the world." It was, he said, "like a feast."

But Clinton had to take part-time jobs to help pay for his costly education. One summer, he went back to Arkansas and worked for Frank Holt, who was running for governor. Holt lost, but his nephew, an Arkansas Supreme Court justice, helped Clinton get a job in the Washington office of Arkansas Senator J. William Fulbright.

Clinton stayed as active as ever in school. He was elected president of both his freshman and sophomore classes at Georgetown. He impressed teachers and fellow students as a focused, hard-working young man. Everyone could see, as one classmate later said, that he was "very political."

Clinton was such a fine student that some of his professors told him to apply for a Rhodes scholarship. Each year, Oxford University in England gives top college students the chance to study there after they graduate. Clinton didn't think he would ever be selected. When he was, he called his mother and asked, "How do you think I'll look in English tweed?"

In 1968, at the age of twenty-two, Clinton graduated from Georgetown and headed off for Oxford. Since his scholarship paid his way, he didn't have to work and could give all his time to his studies. The rich fund of knowledge and culture at Oxford thrilled him. He read more widely than ever, finding many new interests. "I read about three hundred books both years I was there," he said. A friend from those days said that Clinton was "interested in everything."

A crisis was brewing in the United States while Clinton was at Oxford. America was fighting a war in Vietnam. Officials said the war had to be won to stop Communists from taking over all of Southeast Asia. But many people opposed the war. Some said the United States could not win. Others said it was wrong to fight because Vietnam was no threat to our security.

Some young men refused to serve in the military when they were drafted, which was a crime. Others looked for legal ways to avoid service. Clinton had a student deferment—permission not to serve until he finished his studies. He strongly believed the war was wrong and even helped organize protests against it while in England. When his deferment ran out, he took his chances in the draft lottery. In this system, young men's birthdates were drawn by lot. Only those born on the earliest dates picked were drafted. Clinton's birthdate was one of the last picked, so he was not drafted. His escape from service seemed honorable. But details of it would come back to haunt him.

Although Clinton was happy at Oxford, he chose to leave after two years, one year short of getting a degree. He left to take a scholarship at Yale Law School. Getting a law degree was a big part of his long-term plan to enter politics. Many of Clinton's professors at Yale had served in the government under John F. Kennedy. That sort of legal work—public service—was exactly what Clinton had in mind.

One of Clinton's classmates at Yale was a smart, pretty young woman whom he found himself staring at in class. He was afraid to talk to her. But one day, she walked up to him and spoke. "Look," she said, "if you're going to keep staring at me, and I'm going to keep staring back, I think we should at least know each other. I'm Hillary Rodham."

Clinton would soon call Hillary "the smartest person I've ever known." Before long, they were a couple. In 1972, they both took time off from Yale to work on the presidential campaign of George McGovern. Although McGovern lost the election to Richard Nixon, the campaign taught the young law students a lot about big-time politics.

Graduates of Yale Law School were always in demand. After Bill and Hillary graduated, both were offered good jobs in Washington. They were asked to work on the staff of the House Judiciary Committee. It was looking into the possible crimi-

Bill met his future wife, Hillary, at Yale Law School.

nal involvement of President Richard Nixon and his aides in what was known as the Watergate scandal. Most new lawyers would have jumped at the chance to work there. Rodham took the job. But as for Clinton, his next stop was Arkansas.

Back in *1967*, when twenty-one-year-old Bill Clinton was still a student at Georgetown, Roger Clinton was dying of cancer. Bill often made the long drive from Washington to visit him. He wanted to make peace with his stepfather before the end came. "I think he knew that I was coming down there just because I loved him," he later said.

After six weeks, Roger Clinton died. Bill had lost another father. He had never really gotten over the loss of William Blythe, who died at the age of only twenty-nine. That tragedy made young Bill think about when he himself might die, something most children never do. It was one reason he always seemed in such a hurry. "I thought I had to live for myself and for him too," he said.

When Clinton got back to Arkansas, it might have seemed he was slowing down. He did not want to work for any big city law firm. He was happy to be in Arkansas, one of the poorest states in the country. He told his mother that he planned to "break his back" helping his state to prosper, if the people would let him.

Clinton learned that a teaching job was open in the Law School of the University of Arkansas at Fayetteville. But the dean said he was too young for the job. "I've been too young to do everything I've ever done," Clinton said. He was granted an interview—and got the job.

Fayetteville is a little college town tucked into the Ozark Mountains. It was a perfect place for a professor to settle down and enjoy the quiet life of the mind. But Clinton wanted action. Early in 1974, after teaching for only three months, he signed up to run for a seat in Congress. It was held by Republican John Hammerschmidt, who had served eight years and was very popular. Hardly anyone knew who Bill Clinton was.

That would soon change. Clinton ran a dogged campaign. He drove all around in his little car, jumping out to speak to groups of voters wherever he found them. Some politicians found such cam-

Clinton's Fayetteville home during his 1974 campaign for Congress. He lost, but not by much. People began to know his name.

paigning very tiring. Clinton loved it. He didn't expect to win. But he saw the campaign as "an experiment"—a way to learn politics by doing.

Clinton's experiment was a big success. He almost beat Hammerschmidt, who won with only 51.5 percent of the vote. People were stunned. A reporter called Clinton the "boy wonder" of Arkansas politics.

During the campaign, Hillary had left Washington to take a job at the University of Arkansas Law School at Fayetteville. Soon she was managing Clinton's campaign. But she was not sure she wanted to stay in Arkansas. One day, in 1975, while she and Clinton were out for a walk, they strolled by a cozy little glazed-brick house. Hillary said, in passing, that she liked it. Soon, when Hillary was out of town, Clinton went out and bought it. When he sprang his surprise, Hillary was shocked. "So you're going to have to marry me," he said. Two months later, she did.

Clinton had impressed people with his peppy, well-run campaign. Many saw big things in his future. He quickly proved them right. He won election to the post of Arkansas Attorney General in 1976. He was so popular the Republicans didn't even put up a candidate to oppose him.

Clinton was praised for taking on tough issues. For instance, he fought against utility companies to keep them from raising rates unfairly. As his fame spread, many hoped he would seek higher office. He did not let them down. In 1978, he ran for governor and won easily.

At thirty-two, Clinton was the youngest governor in the country when he took office in 1979. He promised to improve education and to bring higher-paying jobs to Arkansas. His goal was to make the state "the envy of the nation."

Clinton launched a sweeping reform plan. His main concern was education. Ever since he was a teenager, he had said that people in Arkansas were just as smart as people anywhere. If they didn't do well in national tests, it was because Arkansas spent less on schools and teachers than most other states. Clinton wanted to raise teachers' pay. But he also wanted new teachers to pass an exam to prove they knew enough to teach. And he wanted to merge

*Bill Clinton was elected governor of Arkansas
for the first time at the age of thirty-two.*

the 382 districts of the clumsy school system into bigger units that would be easier to work with.

Clinton was praised for his energy and intelligence. Even then, some people talked about him as a future candidate for the vice presidency, or even the presidency. But before long, his programs bogged down. Lawmakers would not come up with the money to fully pay for the teachers' raises. People grew angry about merging their hometown school districts with those of other towns. And voters were furious when, to pay for new roads, Clinton raised the fees for car licenses.

Clinton was praised for some of his school reforms. But mostly he faced criticism in the press. His popularity fell. Still, when he ran for reelection in 1980 (Arkansas governors served two-year terms then) most people expected him to win. But the carping about his programs had hurt. He lost a close election to Republican Frank White.

Clinton had looked like a young man with a bright future in politics. Now it all seemed swept away. His mood was dark. What had gone wrong?

He concluded that the people thought he only cared about advancing his own political career. They thought he didn't care enough about them.

Clinton saw that he had tried to do too much, too soon. If he got another chance to serve, he promised himself to take time to explain his programs to the people and win their support.

The man who took Clinton's place was having problems of his own. He had no plan for running the state and was not on top of the issues. He once signed a bill without even bothering to read it first. Some people called him "Governor Goofy."

Clinton was soon back in public view, making speeches critical of Governor White. In February 1982, he said he was running for governor again and that he'd learned from his mistakes. At campaign events, Clinton now asked people to tell him what was on *their* minds. "You can't lead without listening," he liked to say.

Governor White could not run away from his poor record. Clinton won the election. Voters gave him another chance. It was the first time in Arkansas history that a governor who had been beaten won office again.

Clinton, reelected governor of Arkansas, drives slowly through town in a parade with Hillary and their two-year-old daughter, Chelsea.

Education reform was again the main item in Clinton's program. He asked for more money for schools, higher standards for students, and testing for *all* teachers, not just new ones.

Teachers were furious. They said it was not fair to ask experienced teachers to risk their jobs if they failed a test. But Clinton did not back down. He had put Hillary at the head of a committee on educational standards. She helped explain his program to the people. With her help, Clinton convinced them the plan was sound. The legislature passed it into law.

Angry teachers opposed Clinton in the next election. But the public was on his side and he won easily.

By 1988, many people saw Bill Clinton as a man who might be president one day. He had won the Arkansas governorship again in 1986 (a change in the law gave him a four-year term). After that, all his actions were studied for clues to his plans. If he made a speech out of state, reporters said he was trying to build a national following. They expected him to run for president in 1988 and were surprised when he did not.

On July 20, 1988, at the Democratic convention in Atlanta, Bill Clinton gave the speech nominating Michael Dukakis for president. It was a wonderful chance to reach people all over the nation who were watching on television. But everything went wrong. The lights were never dimmed. No one in the hall seemed to be listening. His words were drowned out by chants of "We want Mike!" The speech seemed to last forever. When he finally said, "In conclusion," the hall exploded in cheers, as if the crowd was saying, "Thank God that's over."

Clinton became the butt of jokes. "What a windbag," said talk-show host Johnny Carson. But two nights later, Clinton went on Carson's show, cracked jokes about his speech, and even played a saxophone solo. The audience gave him a big round of applause. "Your saving grace is that you have a good sense of humor," Carson said.

In 1990, Clinton ran for reelection to a fifth term as governor. Voters wondered if he would desert Arkansas in the middle of his term to run for president. Clinton promised to "serve four years" if elected. He won easily again, with 59 percent of the vote.

Meanwhile, Clinton was often in the national spotlight. In 1989, President Bush asked him to be co-chairman of a national meeting of governors to talk about ways to improve education in the United States. In 1990, he was named chairman of the Democratic Leadership Council (DLC), a group of mostly southern party leaders who said Democrats had to change their message to win the presidency.

In the 1980s, Democrats were seen as the party of high taxes and wasteful "big government." Ronald Reagan, a Republican, was elected president in 1980 and 1984, and his vice president, George Bush, was elected president in 1988, by promising lower taxes and "smaller government." But by 1991, Republicans were in trouble. Taxes had been cut, mostly for the rich, who were making more money than ever. But Democrats claimed that the rich did not invest their money to create jobs as much as Republicans said they would—that "trickle down economics" had not worked. Millions were without jobs. And since taxes were lower, the government took in less money and

President George Bush (right) greets Arkansas governor Clinton and Iowa governor Branstad at the opening of the 1989 educational summit meeting.

built up a mountain of debt—over four *trillion* dollars by 1991.

Americans were starting to fear that the nation was in trouble. Democrats thought that if they could shed their "tax and spend" image they could win back the presidency. But probably not in 1992. President Bush was thought to be very popular after leading the way, in 1991, to victory in the Persian Gulf War with Iraq.

Clinton's trips out of state and visits to talk shows fed rumors back home that he would soon run for president. "I'm not running for anything," he would say. But in July 1991, he changed his tune. He admitted, for the first time, that he was thinking about running in 1992. That made many in Arkansas angry. After all, he had *promised* not to run. In September, Clinton toured the state, asking people what they thought. He said that most voters were willing to release him from his promise if he thought running for the presidency would be good for Arkansas and for the country.

On October 3, 1991, Bill Clinton spoke to a large crowd in front of the Old State House in Little Rock. He said that he was running for president because the nation was in danger of losing the American Dream. "The country is headed in the wrong direction fast, slipping behind, losing our way," Clinton told the cheering crowd. Among other things, he called for higher taxes on the rich and tax breaks for people who make investments that create jobs. As he sketched his plan to rebuild the nation, Hillary and his eleven-year-old daughter, Chelsea, stood by his side. But not all Little Rock cheered. One critic wrote that Clinton's broken promise showed that "his word is dirt."

In November Clinton started campaigning in New Hampshire, site of the first presidential primary. Many states held such primaries. In these, voters picked the person they wanted to become their party's choice to run for president. Then that person would run against the choice of the other party. Five candidates besides Clinton were on the Democratic ballot, and one, former Senator Paul Tsongas from Massachusetts, was the early favorite. Few voters this far north had ever heard of the governor of Arkansas.

Clinton announces that he will run for president.

Clinton made a series of speeches about how to solve the nation's problems. Many people were impressed. Here was a politician who spoke with no notes and gave long, thoughtful answers to questions. New stories singled out Clinton as a candidate to watch. Some said he had won the "first primary"—the respect of the press.

On December 15 Democratic delegates in Florida chose Clinton as the winner of a "straw poll" among the six men running. Soon he pulled ahead of Tsongas in New Hampshire. If Clinton could win this far north, many thought he would wrap up the nomination fast. The next bunch of primaries, after New Hampshire, were mostly in southern states. Clinton, the only southerner running, stood to win most of them.

Then disaster struck. In January 1992 a woman named Gennifer Flowers claimed she had had an affair with Clinton and sold her story to a newspaper. Such a scandal can sink a politician's career overnight. Clinton acted fast. He and Hillary went on television to confess that theirs had not been a perfect marriage. But Clinton denied having an affair with Flowers, and said he and Hillary had worked out their problems. What those problems had been he refused to say. It was between him and his wife. "I'm not going to talk any more about it," he said. Then he waited to see what voters thought.

Most seemed to agree that Clinton had said enough. Perhaps voters didn't believe Flowers, who had been paid a lot of money to tell her story. By the end of January, Clinton was back on top of the polls, leading Tsongas 37 percent to 24 percent.

But soon Clinton was hit with another scandal. News reports said he had schemed to avoid the draft in 1969. A letter Clinton wrote while a student at Oxford was read on television. It was filled with a young man's anguish over the war. "One of my roommates is a draft resister who . . . may never be able to go home again," young Clinton wrote. "He is one of the bravest, best men I know. His country needs men like him . . ."

Some said the letter was proof Clinton had dodged the draft. He insisted that was not so. He had been against the war, and he had not wanted to go to Vietnam. But, he said, "I exposed myself to the draft." It was only the luck of the draw in the lottery, he said, that kept him out of uniform.

The scandal raised new doubts about Clinton's character when the old questions were fresh in people's minds. He fell sharply in the polls. It looked as if his campaign might be dying. But Clinton fought on, meeting voters, talking issues.

His persistence paid off. On primary night, he won back much of the support he had lost over the draft scandal. He finished second, with 26 percent, eight points behind Tsongas. It could have been worse. Three men not marked by scandal finished behind him. So at 9 P.M., Clinton did something odd. He called a "victory" party. "New Hampshire, tonight, has made Bill Clinton the Comeback Kid," he said. "I just cannot wait to take this campaign across the country . . . to win the nomination."

The press swallowed Clinton's reading of things. Headlines screamed about his second-place "comeback" right beside Tsongas's actual win. He got a big boost.

Clinton kept campaigning hard. He swept the southern primaries and won other big contests: Pennsylvania, New York, Michigan, and Illinois. By

Above: A few days before the Illinois primary, Bill and Hillary talk to students in the Chicago high school where Hillary was once a student. Clinton says that he will give his wife the credit if he wins there. Right: Clinton reads to children in Washington, D.C.

the time he won California in June, he had the Democratic nomination sewn up. But was he strong enough to beat President Bush, the Republican nominee, in November? Some said he only looked strong next to the weak Democrats he had beaten in the primaries. Polls showed that the scandals had left doubts about Clinton in the minds of many voters. They did not trust him.

But voters were not happy with Bush either. After the glow of the victory over Iraq faded, their thoughts turned homeward. The steady loss of American jobs and the growing mountain of debt made many fear for the future. Bush did not seem to have a plan to turn things around.

The problems of Clinton and Bush made it possible for Ross Perot, a feisty Texas billionaire, to storm into the race. He went on television and said the nation was in crisis and government was ignoring it. Tossing off wisecracks in his down-home Texas drawl, he said government should be run like a business. Perot had never held public office. But since he was very successful in business, millions thought he could fix the nation's problems. It looked as if he could actually win the election.

In late spring, Perot was all over the news. Clinton vanished from television screens and headlines. He crashed to third place in the polls. But much of what was said of Perot was critical. Questions were raised about his business deals. When reporters probed, Perot got testy. Voters began to see another side of him. His poll ratings began to drop.

While Perot was drawing the media's fire, Clinton went doggedly on. He put out a detailed plan to address the nation's problems, and kept reaching out to voters. Slowly, he started to climb in the polls, just as Perot dropped. Then, on the last day of the Democratic convention, Perot suddenly pulled out of the race. Some said he simply could not take the pressure. But many voters were hurt and angry. They felt Perot, who had promised to run, had betrayed them.

Oddly, when Perot broke faith with voters, he handed Clinton a way to cast off doubts about himself. Clinton's dogged refusal to quit when he was under fire now looked like something important—real strength of character.

Clinton seemed to win over many former Perot supporters. By the end of the Democratic conven-

People called the 1992 presidential race "the talk show campaign." Candidates tried to entertain the public more than ever before. Clinton appeared on the Larry King television show and played the saxophone at a club in Washington, D.C.

tion, he had jumped to a huge thirty-three point lead over Bush. Only weeks before, Clinton's campaign seemed doomed. Now he was the clear front-runner in the race for the White House.

Perot's exit had helped Clinton. But so had Clinton's choice of Senator Albert Gore of Tennessee to run for vice president. Gore was a respected expert on defense and environmental policy. Voters saw him as someone who could handle the presidency should something happen to Clinton.

After Bush was nominated at the Republican convention in August, he tried to reawaken voters' doubts about Clinton. Bush, a hero in World War II, reminded voters that Clinton had ducked military service and protested against "his own country" while in England. Republicans used a nickname given Clinton by his political enemies, "Slick Willie," to suggest he was a smooth talker who avoided telling the truth about his draft record and other issues. But voters seemed more concerned about the loss of jobs and the mounting debt. In October, Bush still trailed Clinton by over ten points.

Then the campaign took another twist. Perot said he had "made a mistake" by quitting the race and jumped back in. Bush hoped the Texan would take votes from Clinton. There was a new tension in the race as voters tuned in to watch the three candidates debate each other on television.

During the debates, Perot again amused voters with his feisty wit. But now many saw him as a sideshow, not a possible president. Clinton kept right on plugging his plans to pull the nation out of the rut. As for Bush, he seemed listless, unsure what to say to win voters back. He perked up briefly in the last debate, warning voters that Clinton would bring back the days of "tax and spend." But after the debates, even Republicans said Clinton would be hard to beat.

Bush kept hammering away on the draft issue and character questions. Such tactics tainted Clinton and helped the president make the race closer. But on election day Clinton won, pulling 43 percent of the vote to Bush's 38 percent, while Perot finished a distant third with 19 percent. Clinton carried thirty-two states, and Bush carried the remaining eighteen.

In the second presidential debate, a selected audience asked questions of the candidates. President George Bush talks (left) as Ross Perot breaks in (center) and Bill Clinton looks on.

President-elect Clinton and Vice President-elect Al Gore join hands with their wives to the wild cheers of a crowd gathered in front of the Old State House in Little Rock, where it all began.

The scandals that had rocked Clinton's campaign would have destroyed most others. He survived by keeping focused on issues voters cared about. His victory seemed to mean big changes ahead in America, away from the policies of the Reagan-Bush era. On election night, Clinton saw great things in the nation's future. "With high hopes and brave hearts," he said, standing in front of the Old State House in downtown Little Rock, ". . . the American people have voted to make a new beginning."

How the Country Voted

ELECTORAL VOTES (270 needed to win)

Clinton	370
Bush	168

POPULAR VOTE

43% CLINTON
38% BUSH
19% PEROT

Americans do not vote directly for the President and Vice President. The people in each state choose a group of representatives called the Electoral College to vote for them. To win an election, a candidate must have 270 electoral votes. States have as many electoral votes as the total number of their senators and representatives in Congress. In most cases, all the electoral votes in a state go to the candidate who received the most popular votes.

On January 20, 1993, William Jefferson Clinton took the presidential oath of office on Capitol Hill.

Important Dates

August 19, 1946	William Jefferson Blythe IV (Bill Clinton) is born in Hope, Arkansas.
1968	Graduates from Georgetown University, Washington, D.C. Attends Oxford University, England, on a Rhodes scholarship.
1973	Graduates from the Yale School of Law, New Haven, Connecticut.
1975	Marries Hillary Rodham.
1976	Elected Arkansas Attorney General.
1978	Elected governor of Arkansas.
1980	Loses the governorship to Republican Frank White.
1982	Reelected governor of Arkansas.
1984	Elected for a third term as governor.
1986	Elected for a fourth (four-year) term.
1990	Elected for a fifth term.
October 3, 1991	Announces his candidacy for president of the United States.
July 16, 1992	Accepts the nomination of the Democratic party for the presidency.
November 3, 1992	Wins the election for president of the United States.

Index